Is it the passing of time or the access to more personal time, the acquiring of increased wisdom with advancing years or merely the obsession of ancient mariners, which compels the older citizen to meditate and pontificate?

In a world which is changing - but which is no less interesting and commendable than the 'good old days' - observations, reflections and emotions are still the powerful impulses of living.

This collection is about sharing and caring.

Enjoy!

Thanks

to Michelle and Leanne, Mark, Max and Lori, who tolerate the ramblings of an old man with never-ending patience;

to Betty and my wider family circle who share life's pleasures and pains;

to my many friends - at home, in Hungary, Italy, Norway and elsewhere - who never fail to make me feel welcome as part of their community;

to the staff and artists whom I meet at Annaghmakerrig, all of whom contribute to the recharging of batteries and re-awakening of inspiration;

to David M'Cormick for meticulous proof reading and constructive comments;

to Gordon M'Knight who kindly illustrated the front cover, and the members of Donaghadee Camera Club who provided some of the pictures;

to Angela and John Ley for their sea-faring assistance;

to the writers' groups in Comber and Bangor U3A who keep the creative juices flowing;

and also to you, for taking the time to relax and reflect with me.

Contents

TOMORROW'S PEOPLE

There is my princess
and my young prince too
beautiful angels
with rosy cheeks
and lithesome bodies
expending energy
from lively morning
until innocent sleep.

Emerging from
the chrysalis
of puppy fat
into the wist-
fulness of teenage
beguiling eyes, pure skin
and beautiful hair
so soft and so tender.

I see these things
as you progress
to be always yourselves
so special and
without compare.
I lament the day
when the world opens up
and you fly away.

MY JOURNEY HERE

Retirement makes the days grow shorter
although the task of living stays the same.
The garden grows and hedges never end
and tending them takes for ever in this game;

and the writing bit has filtered in
to add to all the pressures in the frame
as body and mind engage in new pursuits
and fresh images impact upon the brain.

Retirement makes the days grow shorter -
when slower motion could never be to blame
but the garden grows and hedges never end
and tasks take longer still to entertain;

and time is precious to a new degree
as I remember all the things again
that must be squeezed in to these shorter days -
and so I lift my pen and start to write.

KALEIDOSCOPE WORLD

What are the colours in your personal world?
Is happiness orange and is love a bright red?
Is yesterday yellow and is blue for tomorrow?
Is green for summer and purple for sorrow?

Perhaps yours is a world stark and alone
Obsessed by a single monotonous tone?
Or do you see wider, and a vision immense
Where a carnival of colours blazes intense?

Enjoy the new features of diversity living
Cascading like fireworks wherever we look.
Embrace this new world of kaleidoscope cultures
And bring your own colours to this radiant new book.

THE TIDE MILL

SeaGen is a marvel of modern science
as cables and grids full of new technology
will harness the power of the tides
and translate the forces of nature
into new energy to add to
hydro-electrics from waterfalls.

But then there is nothing new in that
and we think of the windmills and wind farms
and even the sails on the ships
that transported people and animals
at a time when continents were still to be found
and the world was thought to be flat.

Long ago someone learned to rub two flints or sticks together
and someone else trundled material on a carted wheel
and in a monastery village at Nendrum
on the same lough of the strong tides
monks were creating a tidal mill to grind their corn
twelve hundred years ago.

SeaGen - a marine turbine installed at the mouth of Strangford Lough in 2009
        to generate electricity from tidal power.

Nendrum - the site of a 7th century Christian monastery on the shores of
        Strangford Lough.
        In the eight century the monks created a tide mill to grind their corn
        - the earliest recorded example of a tide mill.

THE CRAB PARTY

A box of crabs chatters on the back of the bicycle
fresh from the water and testing the air
while the largest of pots simmers and bubbles
eagerly awaiting the gourmet affair.

The ones dead already are thrown to the side
having proved unworthy for the table prepared
for a banquet of eating long into the night
with much singing and talking and company shared.

The youngest of children shriek with delight
as they suck from the claws the softest of meat
while the adults opt for the basket of red
which is richer and dark and a succulent treat.

The novice, bemused, gets help from his hosts
with the cracking and extracting of flesh maritime
declaring a preference for the meat from the claws
while the basket's a pleasure to acquire over time.

FLATLAKE PREPARES

The best part has happened
before the beginning
when the participants will descend
the artists arrive
and the day visitors pour in

for a feast of poetry
and music
and drama
and readings
and anecdotes unending

shared in a setting sun or under a canopy of rain
pattering on the tin roof of a barn
or the taut canvas of a circus tent
as the rich aroma of mouth-watering language
arouses the taste buds of imagination

but now in the silence
of solitude and the sun rising
over a distant golden haystack
the best part has happened
before the beginning

*The Flatlake Festival of Music and Poetry takes place in August
near Clones in County Monaghan*

THE FESTIVAL
were you there too?

The snowy-tops and pony-tails look out of place
in a sea of long-haired androgynous clones
with gothic and emo overtones
swimming and sliding with the current
of yellow and blue and rainbow tents.

The mass of hysteria and musical frenzy
is whipped up by deafening decibels
and cans and needles and cocktails from hell
stimulating abnormal strength
when nature suggests a sleep-debt intense.

As the morning is breaking few are awake
to hear the dawn chorus or see the sun rising
or contemplate eggs and bacon sizzling
to sustain the bodies riddled with mixes
and too many excesses beyond common sense.

When the last song is sung and act performed
and the gig's finally over they flee in their thousands
leaving a litter of debris to distant horizons:
bottles and metal and plastic containers,
and even a sea of discarded tents.

This is the generation of new-age students
and environmental prodigies who
advocate bio-degradable bags and the eco-loo
while they despoil the landscape, and complain of poverty,
and claim more grants for food and for rents.

THE HOODIE

Parkas and i-pods and crowded streets with the bustle of
rush-hour and the crawling fleets of taxis and buses that
transport commuters (who spend half their lives travelling)
home from office blocks and all the pressure where the mind
is numbed as business locks freedom and
family life out of the frame.

Queues that are growing look at watches and start to grumble
at delays in the transport caught in a jumble
with vans illegally parked (just for a moment!) that snare
up the system and frustrate the nerves already jangled
by lights and folk crossing in droves and street vendors: and all
are inescapably trapped.

On an over-crowded bus with many people standing,
his hood over his head and his music loudly blasting,
a youth is oblivious to the hordes that surround him
with his feet and his bag on the seat which is facing him.
His mind is blanked with something that blots out the old woman
standing painfully beside him.

A man taps his shoulder until he gives a shake
with a glazed stare in his eyes that fellow travellers take
as a warning of menace to those in his way.
For a moment all is tied, imitating the slow motion
of the traffic snarled outside, just watching and waiting for
something to happen.

He sees the crowding crisis, jumps up and grabs his bag
and looks wildly with a grimace while others hold their breath
and anticipate some danger.   Then he reaches to the lady
with elegant slim fingers and helps her to the vacant seat
while his discomfort lingers. 'I am so very sorry.
Please forgive me my bad manners.'

A BIG MAN

From the moment we met I admired the man –
cool and decisive and commanding respect
from all whom he met –
except his dog, which refused to respond
to any order he barked (not the dog but the man).

The first meal that we shared with two interpreters,
- although I often wondered how much
he actually understood without them -
was punctuated by many stories of
the tough life on a farm in the country
fifty years before.

The most vivid description I recall quite clearly
as he enjoyed watching me squirm
at the intricate details of a family occasion
when everyone gathered to watch
the ritual slaughter
of a pig that was almost a pet.

And others I will not mention at all.

The simple city boy under the spell of the country giant.

Years later when we met for the annual meal
I recounted the episodes of that first occasion
as I clearly remembered them all –
the pig that was almost a pet
and others I will not mention at all.

Some he remembered and others not –
at least he said that was so.
The pig story was true, others perhaps,
and one he denied to have happened.

Was the simple city boy under the spell of the giant once more?
Was the palinka playing tricks on the mind?
Who was imagining the stories denied –
and rats I will not mention at all?

Palinka - Hungarian plum brandy

MIXED MESSAGES

I am currently reading the teachings of Jain
which hold life as sacred in all that exists
and that even the mining of coal and great metals
is contrary to living a life in God's bliss.

A preacher from Scotland (retired but still active)
who lives in a glen where nature's supreme
suggests in a sermon in Budapest city
that tenement living is part of God's scheme.

A Hungarian girl who is studying life
is shocked that most wars are religion derived
and is happy to say the revival of God
when the wall fell in Berlin was only short-lived.

REALITY LIVING

We have all seen the glossy ads
That take us on the no-
frill flights to cities of our choice.

Many would agree a long weekend with sangria, sun and sea
is better than the same expense for clotted cream and scones and tea
and rain and wind and fish and chips and sand with everything.

You can sample Barcelona with its cocktail bars and beaches
or Paris with the Eiffel Tower and Moulin Rouge and peaches
or Prague with all its history and its special classic features.

The Szechenyi spa in Budapest is amazing to behold.
Where locals play chess in water to their necks from dawn to dusk
while minerals cure their aches and pains and give them skins of hide.

One of the pools has jets of water to massage the body
and a whirlpool to sweep the swimmers round and round in a vortex
that defies their best endeavours to escape and everyone shrieks.

I used to love the power of that current and tried with the best of them
to swim against the force that does not last too long
and so you know that every thing will turn out well.

I do not like it now at all
with its harnessed power
of potential tsunami swell.

THE TAP DANCERS

Tap tap tapping is sounding on the pavement
tapping and laughing is coming down our way
we hear laughing and tapping in the distance
with all the promise of a happiness day.

The tap tap tapping sound is coming closer
and also the sound of laughter starts to swell
the tap tap tapping is a marching drumbeat
and is drawing our attention like a spell.

Suddenly three young men appear together
with one who's leading the rhythm of their walk
they saunter in a sort of dance formation
they're always tapping and laughing as they talk.

First we see the faces and then the bodies
captivating all the passers with the sound
everybody steps aside to let them by
with their white canes tapping smartly on the ground.

One of these three young men is fully sighted
and is telling to the others what they pass
one who is blind from birth is tapping strongly
and the one who's newly-blind is learning fast.

Tap tap tapping passes along the pavement
as they take a learning curve so very steep
with their walking and tapping always laughing
but when he's home again I wonder - does he weep?

CSEREPFALU

Perhaps there were twelve of us there that night
breaking bread and sharing wine at the long oak table
set in a cave carved deep in the mountain
and sharing a mix of English, Hungarian and Hunglish babble.

The chief elder rose and bid us all welcome
and shared his knowledge of the produce with us all
as he lovingly decanted the wines from his cellar
and described the features of each grape in his hall.

In the background the sounds were low and melodic
as the musical brother played folk tunes of old
and captured our spirits with rhythms of history
and haunted our minds with lyrics of gold.

The one who had patiently prepared the goulash
of vegetables, meat, spice, peppers and dill
passed bowls of steaming flavours and fragrances
down the two lines of elders until all had their fill.

The men and the women shared an evening of magic
in talk serious and slight, fun-filled and funereal
and the priest charmed his companions - not with a homily -
but a rich baritone voice that was almost ethereal.

Our musician was asked how he managed such tunes
and played melodiously without recourse to wine.
His response was immediate, sincere and spontaneous -
'Believe in what you are doing and it will be fine'.

There were no moments of doubt in this preparation
which followed a service of anticipation
for a forthcoming eucharistic celebration.
And our faith was the richer that night.

Cserepfalu - a town in northern Hungary

Hunglish - a mixture of Hungarian and English

MISKOLC

Leaving behind the capital city in late afternoon
the train silently bores into the tunnel of darkness,
and through thousands of years of forgotten history
to a destination deep in a cavern of mystery
where streams of thermal waters and perceived images
revive the stories of former dynasties
and a Benedictine monastery in the hillsides of Tapolca.

Emerging in the bright sunlight of a castle yard,
confronted by a richly-coloured tapestry
of knights who joust and roundabouts of merriment
through labyrinths of laughter and the clashing of swords,
while lords in rich attire seek attention and admire
the gracious smiles and elegant styles
of the majestic queens of Anjou.

Passing the haunts of prehistoric Uncle Flint on Avas Hill,
the once Catholic church and tower restored, converted and Reformed;
the broad expanses of Kiraly ut and Jókai Mór;
the vibrant floral beauty of the inner city streets;
the simple lines and cooling fountains of the Heroes Square:
from festivals and concerts to aspic frogs and balls,
and on to Szinva Terrace to meet the Miskolc girls.

Miskolc - a city in the north of Hungary
Tapolca - a suburb of Miskolc
Anjou -   the local royal family in the Middle Ages
Uncle Flint - prehistoric remains found in the area
Kiraly ut and Jókai Mór - the main streets of Miskolc
Miskolc girls - a sculpture in the city centre

CELTIC FIELDS

Against the backcloth of a setting sun
and reaching to a cloudless sky
a relic from a bygone age
focused our thoughts on eternity.

Solitary and still in rural fields
recalling ancient lives in silent form
the Celtic Cross looked coldly down
reminding us of people gone.

The intricate patterns reflect an art
that only living hands could shape
to mark forever the woven lives
of those who sleep.

*This is Muireadach's Celtic Cross at Monasterboice
which dates back to the sixth century and is believed
to be the first of its kind in the country.*

THE TOWER

The group of volunteers step back in history
and give a precious Saturday to idle deeds
found only in the fertile minds
of detached souls rejecting
the incessant pressures of today.

A mediaeval tower set upon a hill
has acted as a landmark beacon
for those who travelled
near and far
across the interval of time.

Today it is the refuge of creative minds
which seek to tease out the dusty corners
of imagination in the archways
and passages and winding stairs
leading up to inspiration.

The iron gate swings firmly shut as the key is turned
for twelve hours of absolute confinement
shared with other searching souls
to record on paper identifying marks
like those ancient scrapings on the walls.

And from this self-imposition of deprivation
emerges a tapestry of unreality, weaving
the battles of history with the frantic juggler
who valiantly copes with modern dinosaurs
and dragons breathing fire.

The day is gone, the work is done.
The pilgrims emerge from grey shadows
And blink at the brightness of the light
as passing children ask their father in hushed tones
if those are the giant's helpers going home.

It is not always easy to set aside the present –
it needs a firm commitment to lonely space
where nature's impulse is free to roam
unhindered by reality. It is the reward
for listening to the silence.

THE CARVING

Who is this person with the half-closed eyes?
Watching our every move from distant time?
Why is our innocent walk on a summer's day
transformed to anxious, furtive, guilty mime?

What ancient culture imposed this curse
with cold uncaring or accusing stare?
Is this the devil wishing us the worst ?
A priest or priestess begging us take care?

Why has this person never smiled?
The thin lips pursed in silent hate?
Because we're here?
Because he's there?
Because of chance?
Because of fate?

One of the pre-Christian figures in the ancient ruins of uncertain
origin on White Island in Lough Erne, County Fermanagh

THE COUNTRY ESTATE

The world drives by the ancient gates
and rarely gets a chance to glimpse
the history hidden up half a mile
of pot-holed avenue lined by untended rhododendrons
dark tree-lined tunnels
and sheep wanting only
the greener grass beyond their fence.

The grandeur of an ancient house
looms large but shows no sign of life
until a small boy guides us in to wait
in a silent room where he and his drawing book and pencil
are dwarfed by the enormous table, high ceiling
and thousands of glass-cabineted books
leather bound dusty and unread for years.

Walking in the close surrounds
the walled garden reveals a selection of neglected implements
and stone busts and frogs and cats and dogs
concealed and watching silently
among the basil, mint and parsley shoots
wildly sharing space with gooseberry bushes
and raspberry canes.

Stone steps lichen covered
lead past an abandoned plough to crumbling houses
and empty stables with broken hinges
that once were filled with the bustle and laughter
of serving families and their happy brood
now existing only in the parish ledgers
and failing memories of old retainers..

FLORABUNDANCE

Flitting lightly through a fantasy of fragrance
from purple fuschia and pink carnations
with bees on lupins and amaryllis
and the rich aroma of honeysuckle

stepping brightly on a carpet of colour
from orange gazama and colourful coleus
with bright yellow sunflowers and candescent campanula
to elegant agapanthus and quivering lilies

and lingering among the shimmering baskets
with fragrant and colourful collections
of exotic blooms and native blossoms
and the silver sheens reflected in evergreens

NOVEMBER IN NORWAY

The darkness of winter's cloak is upon me
as I make my way with barely opened eyes
along the unfamiliar road and silhouetted landscape
of another wet and bitter day

and darkness has returned before I venture back
by those same half-hidden paths
when everything changes to brightness and beauty

as softly the snowflakes
are falling on me.

WAVES

Special memories of idyllic days
walking and resting and enjoying the show
of sand-dunes and pebbles and pieces of driftwood
leading our gaze to the ebb and the flow.

The only real movement is the lapping of water
with gentle waves breaking like pearls swinging on strands
from a distant horizon through small rippling movements
and dispersing like magic on silvery sands.

The hills in the distance are dark but not threatening
a calming dimension over-arching the fair
beauty of nature and making a framework
to both link and divide the water and air.

The sky's a rare blue for this part of the country
and the colluding clouds have a shadowy sheen
as they flit from our feet over water and mountains
weaving the patterns of this special scene.

CURRENTS

Under the surface of the water
mighty currents move unseen
with powerful forces quite concealed
beneath a gentle swell serene.

The daily shoppers in the mall
regard the goods and other folk
with fleeting glances and casual greetings
that stimulate no further talk.

But underneath the calm approach
the deeper inner forces wield
a strong and forceful patent power
and probe strong feelings not revealed.

These chance meetings and greetings and smiles that beguile
behind coffee trays and shop displays
lead to imagined thoughts and acts
the reality of life betrays.

In the lonely minds of some
longing for a hopeful sign
a deeper union opens up
and creates an ecstasy sublime.

Emotions drawn thus together and entangled
merge forever but will never
be one in the days to come
as the currents move in different ways.

SOUNDINGS

after the exploratory moves
as delicate as crystal glass
thoughts deep and unfathomable
move like fragile shells on ocean beds
like tentacles testing new waters

oblivious to established rules
unharmed by tempests tossing far above
unseeing raging storms around
unfeeling fiercest winds about
uncaring and beyond

DEPTHS

It happens in every lifetime
once or twice or more
creating certain feelings
agreeable or sore.

Shadows of greeting
in eyes that are meeting
and some are entreating
a friend beyond fleeting
encounters that fade quickly away.

It may not last forever
be one-sided or two
be lasting or transient
or scarcely noticed at all

but priceless and special
whether silver or lead
to be hoarded and treasured
in the heart and the head.

ECHOES

Those memories will never lose their fatal attraction
as they linger and resonate within the mind
creating a bitter-sweet gathering
of life's encounters and echoing to the end of time
of what is and was and might have been.

The Bora divides idyllic autumn days
from the harsh reality of winter
roaring its chilling avenue
of cold and damp and misty rheum
from Adriatic waters
to the unsuspecting hills
that lie still and supine,
soaking up the last of autumn's warmth
while stripped of summer's foliage
and naked to the ravages of winter chills.

Bora – a cold wind blowing from the Adriatic Sea to the north-east of Italy

FLOTSAM

After the storms and all is quiet
with no hint of the turmoil
which featured
during eighty years of life
we kick aimlessly
among the detritus which litters
the margin of our existence

nothing of value remains
to be seen or shared
with those who follow
to offer inspiration or hope
for a better future
simply placing a burden
of senility and helplessness

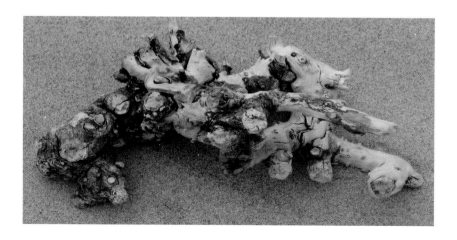

GLOBULES

As children we walked this beach so many times.
It was our playground for the long idyllic summer days
when driftwood became a flotilla of sailing boats
and skimming stones created medallists
at our own Olympian games.

The skimming stones were flat and smooth;
in the movement of wrist and arm the secret lay
and everyone knew the rules of the game –
that most bounces on the water won the day.

Along this very shore we only saw the things
we wanted to see and nothing else –
the wooden craft, the skimming stones,
a dead eel or a stranded jellyfish.

And then we passed the skills to our children
who in turn have educated their offspring
and taught them how to spot the simple things
which bring excitement to a mundane world.

But now I find a new phenomenon on the sands
which has only been there several thousand years -
Mourne granite glistening globules, quite perfect
in their speckled rounded hardness.

The products of eternity of movement,
erosion, friction and nature's sanding.
To my eyes they were not there fifty years ago
just as my grandchildren do not see them now.

RECKONING

They arrived without any warning
With two days 'til the end of the month
And said they would choose sections at random
And begin their audits at once.

Before lunch would be minor departments
And later the secretary's books
Along with the financial controller's
For detailed inspections and looks.

These last two contacted each other
And agreed they must privately meet
For lunch in a pub round the corner
Where their chat could be unheard and discreet.

Ed and Joe had a lot to consider
As they knew the books would reveal
A million pounds of a shortfall
Because of their failed gambling deal.

When Joe went to the toilet after pub lunch
A body lay on the floor
With the pallor of death on his features
And a blade in his hand full of gore.

Beside the corpse was briefcase
Which Joe opened and saw full of notes
Which he realised could cover the shortfall
And even leave some in the floats.

They were back in the office like lightning
And the cash was put in the safe
With a backdated falsification
To give it a valid vouchsafe.

They cleared out their lockers completely
Expecting to be given their cards
And were staggered to hear the M.D. announce
They were in line for some handsome rewards.

- We'll all go out for a meal in the town.
The auditors think we're one in a billion.
The stock market collapse in the morning
Should have cost us all of a million!

YOU'LL STUB YOUR TOE

'You'll stub your toe on that before the week is out'
I told myself as I inspected my room
and then stepped over the raised lintel
on to the balcony with views to lift
the lowest spirit in the land.

In early morning as I stepped gingerly out
the sun was rising over the horizon
of snow-capped hills in the distance
and birds were already singing their welcome
to another crisp Alpine day.

After hours of skiing and sunshine and about
to relax for an hour before dinner
I remembered the danger and was well able to cope
as I sought my seat in the setting sun
with a glass and some crisps in my hand.

Last thing at night before retiring
to rest my healthily exhausted body
after all the fresh air and exercise
I stepped over and out to enjoy
the stars twinkling in the clear and crystal air.

But after the first four days of careful manipulation
on the fifth it was an academic consideration
and instead of my leg in plaster
it would even have been a pleasure
to stub my toe before the week was out.

Annaghmakerrig

ANNAGHMAKERRIG

Here is the big house of Irish writing –
Big, but not the biggest, as we admire
the splendid setting of rural countryside
and the lake just right, located out in front
of the main entrance, with the lawn
sloping downwards to the water
and leading artistic eyes
to rolling hills and woods beyond.

Inside, the rooms are large by modern standards
and the furniture belongs to times gone by
with hand-crafted carvings and human imperfections
deserving more appreciation than our era gives.
Each room is singular, distinct and quite unique
with its own legends of ghosts and unreal happenings
that keep even recent occupants
awake at night.

On crisp and frosty winter mornings
I have heard the bugle calling to the hounds
and listened to the deep-throated baying of the stag
across the fields and dying in my ear.
On stormy days when windows rattled and the rain
beat fiercely down I have looked for Heathcliff
and waited for his shrill demented shouts.
In the calm of tranquil days I have closed my eyes on Innisfree.

This is now the haunt of liberated minds
of those who stretch their imaginative talents
and embrace the ancient lore of traditional arts
together with modern multi-media techniques
within the realms of music, painting, acting and the writing skills.
Writers give the name to painters' pieces,
musicians spot the rhythmic flaws for struggling poets
and players enact all that is around.

We have moved from room to room to watch
developing artistic forms and walked the grounds
to stop under a light or beneath a spreading tree
and witness unfolding drama move from birth to death -
from innocence to argument and separation,
guilt to suicide and retribution,
embryonic thought to wish fulfilment.
The old thespian will be smiling from beyond.

WALK IN THE WOODS

Just after daybreak on a grey morning
tramping a new path through ancient woods
as natural as nature intended
in its raw beauty

A small pool of water in a hollow
where bubbles broke the surface
as I stopped to watch and then discerned
a frog spawning

Spiked stems of wild hawthorn
exposed by the winter's stripping of leaves
suspended the impaled body of
a rat hanging

Logs sawn many years ago
lay uncollected and forgotten
in a pile thickly covered
by moss growing

Disturbed by unfamiliar sounds
of twigs cracking under the feet
of my intrusion
two rooks ascending

HOME FRONT

I was amazed by the stories I heard
from people who said they had nothing to tell –
who apologised for coming and felt in the way
because their role seemed so modest and trivial as well.

We started by giving our names and brief histories
– in a small easy group like old friends who had met
to catch up over tea on the recent events
that had filled our retirement from life's hectic set.

A picture built up as we began to recall
memories triggered by items like an ancient ship's bell
that once summoned the company from duties below –
toasting-forks and horse brasses, candle-snuffers and others as well.

From the child who remembered how Bangor endured
disruption of schooling as classes dispersed
from one building to rooms in various places
including the library attic spaces
– a fragment of history reminiscence unearthed.

The young sisters who lived in number six
which miraculously escaped as the houses nearby
were hit by the random releasing of loads
from enemy planes that were clearing their holds
and pilots returning to base for another day's fix.

There was the story of moving from town into country -
Three sibling children evacuees
to the remote county of Antrim and not fitting in
with a family of strangers not kin:
as foreign as enemies not wanting to please.

The young man who was trained at a military base
in this very town before going to Glasgow
where the basics of guarding were shared
with the locals who mostly stood and stared
and thought that this game was a 'gud little show'.

The English town girl who answered the call
to enlist in the Land Army wielding the tools
- assuming the duties of men taken like cattle -
milking, digging and running an essential battle
in an instant adoption of equality rules.

Another saw service on standby relief
in the north of India where war never reached.
But the Burma connection constantly grew
and readiness was vital as everyone knew
the defences one day might be breached.

The silence was deafening as one told the tale
of being shot down - concentrating the mind -
and placed in a camp in the depths of far Poland
with unspeakable horrors of suffering, and
then describing the guards as 'quite kind'!

Unexpected descriptions which lightened the gloom
that too sombre an outlook might quickly impose
like 'the fun at the bases' and 'good-looking girls'
but youth 'not seeing the dangers' was one of the pearls
that brought our war thoughts to a close.

My views of the war were changed that day
in September, next century, sixty years away…
because the things I read in books and saw on the screen
became real and alive through voices that had been
a history in making – at war, not at play.

VILLAGE OF THE DEAD

We crossed the border at first light
and drove into the dry and dusty hills
where civil war had broken a nation.

The world was eerily beautiful
under a clear blue sky and arid land
that stretched an unreal journey through desert wastes

where only the toughest grasses survived
in fissures where the rocks had cracked
and drops of water might have trickled

in the cold of night when insects scuttled
and darkness revived a semblance of life
in the remnants of yesterday's ravaged homes

razed to the ground.   And the ruins
hid a hundred eyes furtively watching
our every movement from subterranean caves and cellars.

Suddenly round the corner and on a hillside
in a blaze of colour freshly watered and newly tended
generations of villagers huddled together

in the only visible sign of life
in the local cemetery of ravaged history.

I'M TOO YOUNG

I'm too young to remember the war
but I do recall the air-raid shelters
and how I went round and pulled the hair
of mothers and aunts as they lay on the floor
and closed their eyes in silent prayer...

I'm too young to remember the war
but passed those shelters on my way to school
and used the coupons to buy my chocolate
and played with the gas-masks under the stairs
and hated the holes where bombs had cratered ...

I'm too young to remember the war
but every year I feel the power
in November when the poppies fall
to honour the dead –
my uncles and all.

CASTLE ESPIE

See the dappled colours and the piebald patterns.
Watch the mother closely guarding all her numbered brood.
Count the different species as they pass in countless legions.
Spectate as warring siblings scrap for bits of proferred food.

The squabbles end as quickly as they first began
seeming out of nothing like a sudden shower of rain.
Peace descends as quickly as the squawking screaming came
and they all play happy families once again.

The mother duck presides over all that happens out there -
she is diminutive, accomplished articulate and strong.
A leader by her nature and her off-spring rearing history -
her influence and dominance will linger there for long.

The law of the wild is cruel they say
compared to the civilised acts of our kind.
But I see no lingering malice or memory
outliving the lives which fester the mind.

Castle Espie - A World Wildlife Centre at Strangford Lough, County Down

HUMAN RIGHTS

Who are right? - the police and the soldiers
who quell rioting mobs out to destroy?
Or the minority factions which fight
perceived acts of injustice by the 'rule of law'?

Is dictatorship always wrong
and democracy always right?
Or can there be a wrong sort of democracy
and a right sort of tyranny?

Is all life sacred and equal?
Are all humans worthy of similar treatment?
Or are some only fit for destruction
as a threat to the laws we espouse?

There are no snakes in Ireland but the human ones.
And were no values on life in Baghdad.
Genocide rules in many places.
Is 'dog eat dog' good or bad?

It is not a just a question of boundaries
but curbing the excesses of those
whose self-righteous vain glory
always seeks to impose.

My rights exist to the limit of yours
and no further.
No single power prevails
in the common space between.

I will always respect your right to freedom –
just as you must never violate mine.

BEST REVOLUTIONS

The best revolutions
are evolutions
when agreement leads
to new solutions.

A system which devolves
is one which evolves
from bad to better
and better to best.

A mutual promise
is the road to compromise
through accommodation
not repudiation.

NEWCOMINGS

My earliest memories of encounters in Down
relate to the railway long since abandoned
which ran from Belfast and carried our family
to visit relations in Comber.
A happy day's visit included a walk
down the narrow Mill Street and trespassing
for chestnuts by climbing a fence
and avoiding the gamekeepers
loaded with shotguns
who regarded small boys
as vermin to go (or so I was told).

On other occasions with jars in the autumn
we took the bus and sandwiches for lunch
(which we children ate before Belfast was left)
and made our way to Scrabo
and the long and dusty path up to the Tower
which was a rich source of scratches and blackberries
and our fingers and tongues were stained with purple
in the original version of 'PYO'
with which my mother would make pies and tarts
as a special treat for ourselves and our neighbours
and there was always some money inside.

And still I am haunted by the vivid memory
of a Christmas Day with snow on the ground
when I was only eight or nine
and the family was gathering sadly in the country
to lament and bury an elderly aunt
in the family plot on a winter's day of birth and death
but as the funeral procession went round a corner
the wheels of the hearse spun on the ice and slid into a bank
and the men got out to give it a push
while I stayed with my mother and shivered with fear
at the prospect of spending a night in a ditch with a corpse.

LET THE DOG BARK

When we got the dog the family agreed
It would be for life and all would feed,
Walk and play with the hybrid breed
And give it the love it deserved.

The early weeks were fun and games
As we tried to think of suitable names
And it wasn't easy to toilet train
And its puppy teeth were sharp and nipped.

We remember the day it got a fright
When it opened its mouth and did not bite
But barked instead and became uptight
And whimpered with fear of its self.

The bark developed more and more
Becoming soon like a ferocious roar
At the postman, the neighbours, a ring at the door
Until we were fit to be tied.

Our best psychology was rather neat
As friends calling earned the dog a treat
And the postman offered biscuits to beat
The warning barks which were quickly gone.

Soon the sight of a dog or cat,
A bird in the garden or mouse on the mat
Could create no disturbance that
Would raise a bark from the dog.

Even those who came in the dark of night
When we thought our home was locked up tight
And with all of value took their flight
Got only the wag of a tail.

THE UNENDING ROAD

Is it only in my memory
that the youthful adventure of travel takes place
with a carefree departure from formal behaviour
into the regions of freedom?

Six or eight or ten of us crowd
into an ancient wagon much too small
but that in itself is part of the programme
of breaking the rules to be free.

For days we are travelling from here and to there
wherever those places might be
and gone are the thoughts of responsibly living
hidebound and in debt to society.

Long gone are the urban and suburban shadows
into the remotest and wildest of places
as our minds and our actions lose all restrictions
and we find ourselves drifting away.

The desire to escape that had bound us together
is the same force that drives us apart
until we can barely recognise each other
we have travelled so far on the way.

My journey now is long and alone
and no end is in sight wherever I look

THE INHERITANCE

I had forgotten about this box
and what it contains.
I last saw it thirty years ago
when I was tidying up
and put it away in the roofspace.

When my time has come and then has gone
and my children are filling black bags for the skip
perhaps they will find this and wonder.

A small black and white box and its contents.
Will they shake it and rattle it
and ask what it is?

Perhaps they'll be sorry
when it is opened –
no diamonds, no silver,
not even a watch.

Should I write a short note to put with it?
And say that this ammonite is rare and unique?
That a museum would be proud to display it forever?
And generations would marvel and ponder?

Perhaps I should tell of the strangest events
that led me to find it on the wildest of beaches,
the romance and the mystery that had taken me there.

But I think I'll say nothing at all.
The fossil and its history can die with me
when the box and a bin-bag unite in a dump.

It is my story, my history, my lodestone or star.

DISTANT CORNERS

From distant corners of my dreams
I see the ambitions of my life
which prompted all the energy
that flowed in never-ending streams.

The early inspiration was
the thoughts of what might be the goal;
the search for elevated aims
to justify each worthwhile cause.

The middle years of life perceived
that happiness matters most of all
for self and others – not crusades
for principles that few believed.

And now advanced in twilight years
those dreams seem distant futile thoughts -
but I give thanks with all the rest
for a life more of laughter than of tears.

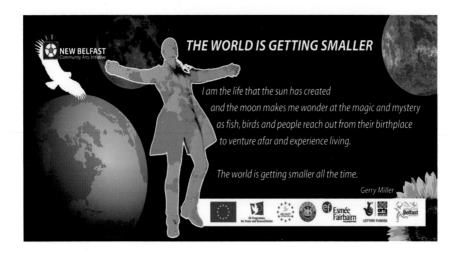

THE WORLD IS GETTING SMALLER

The world is getting smaller all the time.

I am the sun that circles the world
giving the heat and making the life
of the fish in the waters and birds in the air
and the people who live on the land.

I am the moon that shines all the time
reflecting the light of the sun in dark places
making mystery and romance and pulses of wonder
in the minds of the life that the sun has created.

I am the life that the sun has created
and the moon makes me wonder at the magic and mystery
as fish, birds and people reach out from their birthplace
to venture afar and experience living.

The world is getting smaller all the time.

OBLIVION

Feeling a little light-headed
I make to sit on the bench
for a moment
but do not make it

and open my eyes to see two strangers
inserting a drip
and gently wiping
my blood covered face

and passers-by looking
as the paramedics
ask for my name and say it was good
that someone had dialled for help

and the interval could have been
seconds or minutes
which never existed and
were lost from my life

and awareness was thinking
that if this was like
the oblivion of death
then it is nothing to fear

WHEN YOU RETIRE

'... and now, my friend,
enjoy the luxury of living
surrounded just by those you love;
eclipsing from your daily rote
all thoughts of sycophants and servile minds
that steal the precious pearls of time.'

44   *Annaghmakerrig*
The family home of Tyrone Guthrie (1900-1971) in County Monaghan
is now a retreat and residential centre for writers and artists.

48, 51   *'Home Front'* and *'I'm Too Young'* first appeared in *'Memories of Bangor'*
ISBN 1 89898820 X

61   *'The World is Getting Smaller'* was selected as one of the first five poems
featured as part of the Belfast Metrobus *'Poetry on the Move'* collection.
The illustration is by Steven Tunley of New Belfast Community Arts.

Front Cover Painting by   Gordon M'Knight, Donaghadee Camera Club

Photograph Acknowledgements

15   *The Crab Party*   Paul Miller, Donaghadee Camera Club

36   *Currents*   Danny M'Caughan, Donaghadee Camera Club

37   *Soundings*   Mollie McConaghy, Donaghadee Camera Club

38   *Depths*   Paul Miller, Donaghadee Camera Club

39   *Echoes*   Alan Neville, Donaghadee Camera Club

*For thirty-five years Gerry Miller taught English and English literature .   He was awarded
a Churchill Fellowship to engage in educational research in Australasia, was a founder committee
member of the Northern Ireland Council of Christians and Jews, and is a member of the executive of
The Peace People (founded by Nobel Peace Prize Laureate Mairead Corrigan Maguire).*
*Now he lectures extensively in Denmark, Hungary, Italy and Norway as well as Australia, India
and north America, offering a unique collection of lectures and talks about the island of Ireland, based
upon a lifetime's experience of its culture and communities.*
*His academic credentials include degrees and awards in English Literature and Ecumenics. His first
collection of poetry 'Awakening' ISBN 0-9548251-0-1 was published in 2004*
He is a member of the Irish Writers' Union and Irish Pen.